# BATTLEFIELD HOPE

# BATTLEFIELD HOPE

Lessons from 30 Years

of Surviving Cancer

*A Memoir and Guide for Patients and Families*

Susan Brearley

Garden of Neuro Institute Publishing

*Battlefield Hope: Lessons from 30 Years of Surviving Cancer*

A Memoir and Guide for Patients and Families

Part Two of this book was originally published in 2006.

ISBN: 978-1-962077-20-0

Published by

Garden of Neuro Institute Publishing

First Edition: December 2025

*For Russell*

*My Zen master son*

*who was nine months old when I was supposed to die*

*and who has been teaching me ever since*


*And for Nana and Poppy*

*Who showed me what it means to live fully*

*on a hilltop in Montserrat*


*And especially for all the patients and supportive friends, and*

*families who never give up hope*

# CONTENTS

# PART ONE

*Thirty Years Later*

# I Am From

I am from Reading, Pennsylvania—the same home of John Updike, Keith Haring, Wallace Stevens and Taylor Swift. I am from the school of not being a fan of Reading, Pennsylvania.

I am from Grandma Becker's house with the giant silver gazing ball and the non-stop yard, that who knows now who mowed all the way back to the tree line—so far that even the strongest child running got tuckered out.

I am from my Aunt Jane who always asked if I wanted her to make me my favorite cream cheese and apple butter sandwich and I never said no.

I am from the Amish and Mennonite families, the horse and buggies that parked across the street and "Mom, I'm going out to feed the horses."

I am from music—opera, Broadway, church choirs and county choruses. A mom who trained as an opera singer and sang to us every day of her life until the cigarette smoke finally stopped her.

I am from one father who drank too much and another who laughed and way-too-often was running off, chasing fire.

I am from dance—tap, Cajun, contra, lindy hop, Schottische, salsa, merengue, hambo, tango, Scottish country and Appalachian clog dancing.

When Nana and Poppy moved to the Caribbean, I became from there—from hibiscus, grapefruits, mangos, and bougainvillea, puffy mile-high clouds, and the wild donkey in the field that brayed for the carrots in our pockets as Poppy and I approached on our morning walks around the bend.

I am from the kaleidoscope that sat in Poppy's Kutztown, Pennsylvania, library, and the glass chips that dropped on every turn, showing me the way to be the seed of hope and the harvest in the next generation; how to be the rainstorm of rebellion and the peaceful joy in a life well lived.

❧

That's where I come from. But this book is about where I've been since—and how I'm still here to tell you about it.

*Thanks to George Ella Lyon for the inspiration to write my own I Am From poem.

# The Diagnosis

In 1995, after a routine visit to my regular family doctor, I was referred to an oncologist for a biopsy.

Days later, I was sitting in their office, hearing a pronouncement that I had inflammatory breast cancer. The prognosis was not good, and I needed immediate surgery.

That week was a whirlwind of activity. The tumor was huge, a breast and 32 lymph nodes under the arm were removed, and 28 were found to be positive for the cancer. It was a certainty that it was all over my body, floating around in my bloodstream, waiting to attach to other organs.

With a straight face, the doctor told me I had 6 months to a year to live.

My son, the Zen master, was 9 months old at the time.

I told the doctors, "You don't get to tell me that. You don't get to tell me how long I will live. I am a mother with a 9-month-old child. He needs his mother."

In 1996, before Google and the internet had become the tremendous research engines they are today, I became determined to become my own research project.

The project was "Save My Own Life."

My manager at IBM told me to take all the time off I needed. I was given a year, with full pay, to fund my project. I would have been without pay after 12 months. This level of corporate generosity is unprecedented in today's economic climate.

Immediately after my surgery, I booked a flight to the Caribbean to spend a few weeks with my grandparents. They lived on the tiny island of Montserrat.

The doctors tried to shame me into not taking that trip. They said I was jeopardizing my treatment. They had plans for high-dose chemotherapy and radiation therapy.

I told them I was leaving and would speak with them upon my return.

The words swirled around me, and I needed to ground myself. My safe space was always with my grandparents, and that was where I headed.

❧

# Montserrat

My grandparents had retired and lived on the island of Montserrat for 30 years, in this absolutely pristine paradise of a tiny island nestled in the Leeward chain of the Caribbean.

During my 27-year career at IBM, I spent all my vacation time there, as much as I could manage. Montserrat was my spiritual home—but really, that home could have been anywhere they were.

My grandparents loved entertaining. Tea parties, afternoons playing bridge, full dinners, Caribbean sunset viewings, and "Adventures in Listening"—they never missed an opportunity to gather and socialize.

Phones would ring across the island as my grandfather carefully watched the weather reports for a clear sky. "There's a green flash happening tonight," he'd tell my Nana, and she'd set up in the kitchen to bake bread, or a clafouti, or delicate finger sandwiches, after they decided to invite others to see this rare optical spectacle. The sun, in its last throes, would gently depart with a brilliant green flash at the last moment of dipping under the water.

And so, because they were known to all as great hosts, the governor rang them up one day.

"There's a Royal Navy ship mooring this week, would you like to entertain some officers?"

"Why of course!" came my grandmother's reply, and she planned for a full dinner on her best fine china.

About a half hour prior to the appointed arrival, my grandfather heard a rustling in the bushes outside. He investigated, seeing that it wasn't the usual free-roaming cattle or donkey.

He went to the kitchen. "It must be someone important," he announced. "Look! Secret Service." I can still hear his child-like, understated whisper, which was characteristic, especially when he was emphasizing excitement.

When the officers arrived, three officers introduced themselves, including Prince Charles.

After dinner, he excused himself from the table and came to the kitchen, where my grandmother was cleaning and preparing dessert.

"May I have a look in your pantry?" he politely asked.

My grandmother kept a well-stocked pantry. On a tiny island, you never know when the next supply ship will arrive.

"Of course!" she replied with enthusiasm. And when he pointed to a jar and asked, "What is this?" she reached up to the shelf and said, "Oh, you don't know apple butter?" And in her best Pennsylvania Dutch-trained hospitality, she cracked open the jar, grabbed a spoon, scooped out a giant dollop of the delicious cinnamon-y paste, and handed it to him.

And so it was that Prince Charles had his first taste of apple butter in my grandmother's pantry.

This was where I went to heal. This was where I found my answers.

§•

I spent those weeks meditating, practicing yoga, and reading old nutrition books from my Nana's personal library. They were her resources for keeping my grandfather alive, with all his health issues. That was why they had originally moved to the island—to keep him alive.

One book on her shelf changed my life. It described a study where researchers gave mice cancer and then effectively cured them—no recurrence—with vitamin A dosages. That book is why I would later juice pounds of carrots every day until my palms turned orange. The doctors were not happy about it. But I had done my research.

While in that silence, peacefully ensconced on a hilltop with the sounds of the surf surrounding me constantly, I would go for daily walks with my grandfather, feast on my grandmother's fresh fruits and veggies from her tropical garden, and develop a plan for myself—a plan for healing.

৶

When I came back to the United States, people thought I had gone a little crazy. Doctors continued to accuse me of sabotaging their treatment plans.

I interviewed a parasitologist from the University of Texas who shared research that convinced me I needed to do regular parasite cleanses. I paid over a thousand dollars to import a water alkalizing machine directly from Japan—there were no distributors in the United States, and no one knew what it was for. I had read about the thoroughbred horses in Lexington, Kentucky, and how they all drank water from the naturally alkaline limestone water table, which strengthened them. Dr. Batmanghelidj's book about water was another powerful motivator.

I juiced and drank carrot juice until my palms turned orange. The doctors became angrier with me. They thought I was crazy. I did not care. I was determined and armed with my research.

*"When they call you crazy, that's code for 'keep going.'"* —*Kyle Cease*

People around me thought I was dying. That is what the doctors told everyone was going to happen.

I was not convinced they were the ultimate authority about my life.

☙

# When I Didn't Die

When I didn't die, people were shocked. I had radiance and energy after the ordeal that prompted one of my sisters to say, "You look better than me, and you're the one that's supposed to be sick!"

And it was true. I was glowing. I had been a vegan for a year and ate no cooked foods. No meat, lots of tofu, though, much to the dismay of my husband at the time. That certainly was one of the things that caused him to decide to divorce me. Tofu—one of the last straws for many.

A few years after I, and everyone else, realized that I was not going to die according to the predictions of the smartest and best paid doctors I had at my disposal, thanks to a full medical insurance paid for by IBM—I began to tell my story in public gatherings—at church groups, reading circles, women's clubs, or any place I was invited to speak. I spoke in states all over the country.

At one of these gatherings in Florida, I was approached in the parking lot by a very large black man named Leon. He was the size of a football player. I was worried I had said something wrong.

He simply looked at me, and said, "TELL YOUR STORY."

I had thought that was what I had been doing. I think I must have felt timid in front of my audience.

But what I realized that day was that when we tell a story, sometimes we think we are telling it for ourselves. To benefit us in some way. Maybe it's a catharsis, maybe it's for money, or for any other reason, one of the many reasons we tell ourselves the story is important.

You never know who will read or listen to your story and be touched. You just don't know who will be inspired. And for that person who is supposed to read or hear your story, your words can mean everything. They can be a turning point.

In 2005, while I was still alive after this ordeal, ten years later, after they predicted my demise, I took a retreat to a beautiful space in my backyard—Mohonk Mountain House. There, I wrote a little book and self-published it. KDP wasn't even a thing until 2007. I called it Battlefield Hope.

That book is what you'll find in Part Two of this edition. I've preserved it exactly as I wrote it then—a woman ten years past her terminal diagnosis, trying to share what she'd learned with others who might be facing their own battles.

But now it's thirty years later. And I have more to tell you.

# The Years Between

What does survival actually look like? Not the dramatic moment of being told you're going to die, or the triumphant moment of being told you're in remission. I mean the years. The decades. The Tuesday afternoons and the January mornings and the ten thousandth time you wake up in a body that was supposed to be dead by now.

I had three husbands. Each marriage taught me something, and each ending contributed to who I am today. I used to say my relationships were unsuccessful. Now I know better. They were all successful, because I'm still here, still learning, still capable of love.

I raised two sons. One of them—the nine-month-old baby who needed a mother—grew into what I call my Zen master. He's thirty now. We laugh together before surgeries. We quote Monty Python in hospital waiting rooms. He understands impermanence in his bones.

The other son, the older one—that's a harder story. There's an estrangement there, and I don't see my grandchildren. I've learned that there are some things in life for which you may never find resolution. You carry them. You don't let them poison you. You keep the door open, and you keep living.

And then my body started falling apart in new ways.

# Body Parts

## A Poem

*I shouldn't be so surprised. I've lost body parts before.*

Back when I was a wee girl, when everything was magical, and parents and teachers and grandparents all romanticized about tooth fairies—faces lit up when they saw my naked gums, where just before a baby tooth lived.

It was a rite of passage, losing those teeth. An accomplishment, rewarded with coins and candy.

So, why now does losing a breast not get rewarded?

Why do we not light up when someone says, "I lost my breast today," and then there's a breast fairy who brings you a new Mazda Miata convertible as a reward?

It would make the whole ordeal so much easier and fun. Something to look forward to.

❧

July 2019 will go down in history as my least favorite month that year, or most any year. It's then that my boob exploded.

Let me back up.

24

I was cleaning an Airbnb—one of the ways I pay my bills so I can invest in what I call the Bank of Susan: reading, writing, meditating, walking in nature, eating delicious food. Everyone has to pay their bills.

In the kitchen drawer, I found a silverware display tray cable-tied to its cardboard box. Not lightweight cable ties—thick industrial strength ties, meant for big, thick, beefy tie-up jobs. I grabbed a knife to cut them loose.

The knife bounced off the cable tie and sliced my wrist.

My entire left hand immediately went numb. The whole thing.

I fumbled for my phone and dialed 911. I told them I cut my wrist. They asked me if it was an accident. Because that needs to get out of the way first, I guess.

Every single medical professional that night asked me if it was an accident. I couldn't stop laughing. It was the stupidest of accidents. And the irony was that everyone in my kitchen who helps me as a sous chef gets the constant drone from me about knife skills and safety.

By some miracle, not a single blood vessel was cut. But nerves were.

The entire month of July, the hand and forearm were a seething mess of nerve issues—feeling like pins and needles, hot pokers stabbing, weird, indescribable mystery pains that would just come and go. I was beginning to resign myself that I would not have use of my left hand ever again.

And then, at the end of July, just when I thought nothing else could go wrong, my boob exploded.

Okay, not a real boob. I'm a breast cancer survivor, and I wear a prosthesis. This fake boob is made of silicone stuff. And I guess it just served its purpose, reached its date for planned obsolescence, and the seam broke loose. When I took off my bra, there was silicone residue all over my bra, my clothes, and my chest. Sticky, like chewing gum.

Imagine if that silicone had been inside my body.

So yeah. July was not a great month. But I learned to type again with dead fingers. I got my sailing certification one-handed. I kept writing, even when haiku was all I could manage.

What else are you going to do?

ॐ

# The Second Cancer

I'll admit I was a scaredy cat about the colonoscopy. I was supposed to get one much earlier, but I kept putting it off. I didn't do my first one until I was sixty-six.

They found a massive polyp. So large that the gastroenterologist couldn't remove it during the procedure. She gave me options: see a specialist more experienced with difficult polyps or go straight to surgery. Surgery seemed smarter. If another doctor tried the scope and failed, they'd wake me up and put me back under anyway.

Part of the problem was location—the thing was lodged right near the ileocecal valve, where the small intestine meets the large, nestled up against the appendix.

The risks were serious. I could lose significant portions of my GI tract. I could wake up with a colostomy bag. Infection was a real possibility. This was not a minor procedure.

When I met with the surgeon, he showed me exactly where the polyp sat. Right there, next to the appendix.

"Hey," I said, "since we're going in anyway, why not take the appendix out too? Free with purchase, right?"

He agreed.

That summer, I had the surgery. Scared doesn't quite cover it, but I'd faced worse odds before.

In the post-op appointment, the surgeon delivered the pathology results.

The polyp—that massive thing that had driven this whole ordeal—was benign.

The appendix, on the other hand.

They'd found cancer. A small, contained tumor. A type that stays put. And they'd got it all.

"Congratulations," he said, essentially. "You're cured of cancer."

A cancer I didn't even know I had.

I walked out of that office with a strange, familiar feeling settling into my bones—a feeling I'd had before, thirty years earlier, when I'd somehow survived what should have killed me. The feeling that my work here on this planet is not yet done.

એ

# At the Hospital

I never in a million years thought I would work at a hospital. Who would, unless that was your career? It's a scary place where most people do not wish to go.

But in truth, working at the front reception desk, I get to practice all the Buddhist precepts—grace, compassion, and being present for people in some of their darkest and most challenging moments.

People are having babies, celebrating being grandparents or aunties for the first time. Others are being wheeled in on wheelchairs, coming for a life-saving procedure or surgery, or trying to find their loved one in the emergency room. Still others are going to the ICU, or a hospice room, where their family member or best friend lies actively dying.

I watch families rush in at the last minute before visiting hours end. "Yeah, we know we're late, but we're just here to say good night to Mom in the last few minutes." Their mother has been in the ICU for the past week. We badge them in, saying, "Of course!"

I reflect on these moments for days. How dedicated those families are to take a long drive for just a few minutes with their possibly dying mother.

And then there are the moments that break you open.

It was 5:30 in the morning. A man appeared at my desk. He was shaking. He couldn't breathe properly. His wife had just died.

I asked him, "What do you need?"

He looked at me with eyes that were still in shock, still processing what had just happened in the room he'd walked out of, and said, "I don't know what I need."

There are no right words for that moment. There is no protocol in the employee handbook. There is only presence.

I went around the desk and hugged him.

He left sobbing, walking outside to smoke a cigarette.

This is the actual work of a hospital reception desk. Not just badging people in and giving directions. Being present when someone's world has just ended. Offering human contact when there are no words that will help.

I watch nurses, young and old, keeping patients comfortable, safe, and helping them heal. The president of this hospital is a woman. Most of the people doing the actual work of keeping others alive are women.

Before they wheeled me into the OR for my arm surgery, I stopped everyone.

Two anesthesiologists and the nurse paused mid-stride. My Zen master son looked up. Four faces, suddenly attentive in that fluorescent-lit hallway where a thousand gurneys have rolled toward a thousand surgeries.

"I'd like to take a moment," I said, "to tell you how grateful I am for you and this team. You probably get taken for granted a lot. But I recognize that you've spent years of training to help other people have better lives. I am grateful for you."

They stopped in their tracks. Really stopped—the way people do when they've heard something unexpected. The lead anesthesiologist said Thank you. Then, as he began wheeling me toward the operating room, he started asking questions. What do I like to do in my free time? Where do I go? What brings me joy?

They seemed stunned, as if no one had ever done something like this before. I think these teams should hear gratitude more often.

෬

# Looking Forward to Pain

I'm a two-time cancer survivor. The mastectomy was in 1995. The appendectomy was last summer. December brought a dislocated ankle with a minor fracture. Then came the arm surgery—another operating room, another moment of uncertainty before anesthesia erases the world.

I've learned what these moments cost.

So when my surgery started three hours late—3 PM instead of noon—I watched other people's faces tighten with frustration in the waiting area. But my Zen master son and I? We had extra time to laugh.

We joked about my hesitation to hand over my living will during check-in. "I've got organ donation on there," I told him. "You know that Monty Python sketch where they show up at the guy's door while he's still alive, ready to harvest his organs because he signed the form?" We were laughing about them making some unfortunate decisions while I was under.

Then the conversation turned to luxury—this new hospital with its modern appointments, comfortable spaces, and good lighting. "Luxury!" my son said, and we were off into the Four Yorkshiremen sketch. "When I was young, we lived in a shoebox in the middle of the road!" We spent the next hour competing over who had the more absurd childhood memory, laughing until the nurse came to say it was time.

I kept thinking: isn't this a nice memory to have? The last time you might ever talk to someone you love, you're laughing and telling stories and having a good time. Wouldn't it be nice if life were always like that?

The morning after surgery, I was watching the sunrise from my hospital bed. Most people prefer rooms on the other side of the hospital—the ones with glorious views of the Hudson River. This side has a view of the parking garage and the parking lot.

But this side also has the sunrise.

Gray and blue and yellow, bright and cheery. Nothing dramatic—no explosive pinks or oranges—just light arriving to announce the day. The day is here. I am here.

Most people prefer the vista. I got the light.

The anesthesiologist had given me a nerve block, which helps with pain but also deadens the nerves that control motion. My right arm felt the way it feels when you fall asleep on your arm and wake up to find the entire limb gone—no feeling, no control, just dead weight attached to your shoulder.

I told the nurse that morning that I was looking forward to the pain.

She looked at me like I'd lost my mind.

But pain means recovery. Pain means I still have an arm to feel with. Pain means the nerves are waking up, the body is healing, and life is returning to tissue that was temporarily silenced.

Somewhere, someone woke up today with no arm to wake up. I get to complain about mine hurting. That's not suffering. That's privilege.

❧

# Good Night Mom

On August 6th, in the middle of the day, I received a phone call from a funeral director in Pennsylvania, where I come from. Funeral directors do not randomly call people out of state.

"What's the recorded date of death?" I asked.

"July 31st," he replied, and then immediately apologized to me after realizing that he was the one notifying me that my mother had passed.

My sisters had not told me she had died.

The last conversation I'd had with my mother had been on the telephone, over five years earlier. Her brother Tom had died. I called to express my condolences. She was a gifted storyteller, and she began telling me funny stories of the siblings as children. Then, rapidly, her stories and eventual accusations turned into anger over my grandmother's final wishes. She hung up the phone on me.

I tried reaching out afterwards. She never responded.

A friend once told me, there are some things in life for which you may never find resolution.

I searched online for any news about my mother's death. I found an obituary, bare bones—a sparse few sentences. It said she died in the local hospital. She had been a chain smoker her whole life. Smoking finally killed her voice. Perhaps it finally got her in the end.

The obituary said, in lieu of flowers, send a donation to the American Cancer Society.

The obituary said, Funeral services will be at the convenience of the family. That is code for "there will be no funeral services."

I tried looking for phone numbers for my sisters to call them. I found one on Facebook. I sent a private message saying I was curious about what happened and the story about Mom's passing.

She sent me an emoji—👍—the most passive-aggressive of all emojis.

There is a price to pay for living in New York, or any city. The cost of living is high. Food, taxes, utilities—all cost more than double what they cost to live in a small town.

I willingly pay this toll to live in a place where I know I will be constantly surrounded by unique experiences, travelers, artists, poets, and storytellers who share their lives with each other. Willingly, enthusiastically, delightedly.

The cost of leaving the countryside where I was born is the painful reality that I will forever be ostracized as not belonging to the community, because I chose to leave it.

For now, all I can do is write and tell my stories.

For now, all I can do is write—

Good night, Mom.

෨

# Drop It

My grandmother—Nana—was a force. In an era when women were expected to choose between career and family, she did what she had to do to survive a difficult first marriage, then went back to school and got her doctorate in Clinical Child Psychology. She remarried a widower who adored her ferocity and perseverance of spirit, and supported her through her journey. That was my Poppy.

They moved to Montserrat for his health and stayed for thirty years. They hosted Prince Charles and green flash viewings and a lifetime of adventures.

But one day in her Caribbean kitchen, when we were taking care of the dinner dishes—she was about in her late 70s by then—she started to talk about her father.

For years, I had heard the stories of her father. There was no doubt in my mind: the experience she had, of struggling with someone she had to fight with every step of the way, had served her in a way that wasn't pleasant, but did create the motivation she needed to survive and thrive.

The stories she shared about her father were few, but they always had a negative tone. She clearly harbored a feeling about him. It was decidedly not a feeling of gratefulness. She held onto this anger for years.

On this particular day, something inspired me, and I asked her one simple, curious question: "Nana—how long will you be staying angry at your father?"

She stopped washing the dishes. She turned and looked at me. I could see her facial expression change, and in fact, her entire body posture transformed. It was as if she had just dropped a very heavy load of invisible luggage she had been carrying around for decades. She looked lighter.

She didn't say a word. But I witnessed the transformation the second she had the epiphany. She had been carrying something around for years that no longer served her—it was no longer needed. And just like that—she let it go.

And all the stories she shared about her father from that point on were filled with love, gratefulness, and joy. The stories had been inside all along. They were just masked with a veil of hurt, turned into anger.

What luggage from the past are you carrying around that you absolutely no longer need?

How long do you intend to carry it?

Just let it go.

❧

# Why This Book Now

I wrote the original Battlefield Hope in 2005, ten years after my terminal diagnosis. I wanted to share what I'd learned with others who might be facing their own battles.

The world has caught up to what I was doing in 1995.

When I was diagnosed, I paid over a thousand dollars to import an alkaline water machine from Japan. Now you can buy alkaline water at any grocery store. When I was searching for information about alternative treatments, I had to track down obscure research papers through interlibrary loan. Now you can find almost anything with a Google search. When I was looking for support, I had to find local groups. Now there are online communities for every type of cancer, every type of treatment, every stage of the journey.

Meditation apps didn't exist. Now there are dozens, including some designed specifically for cancer patients. Yoga classes for cancer survivors didn't exist in my small town. Now they're everywhere, and you can also find them online.

I created an email address back then— wiseamazonwoman@yahoo.com—my first email outside of IBM. I was scared the company might fire me for having a personal identity online. These were the early days of the internet. I still use that email today.

This is what a life looks like on the other side of a death sentence.

When I was a little girl, cancer was a death sentence. You didn't talk about it. People whispered the word. If someone got it, you prepared for the funeral.

It's not that anymore.

Dr. Viktor Frankl survived the Holocaust and wrote about it in Man's Search for Meaning. Dr. Edith Eger, his student, was a sixteen-year-old girl in Auschwitz and is still teaching today—her book The Gift should be required reading for anyone facing the impossible. Psychologist Dan Gilbert studies what he calls our "psychological immune system"—our remarkable ability to recover, adapt, and find meaning.

What all of them understand is this: our ability to hold hope and envision our future self is the thing that propels us forward. If you can see it, you can reach for it.

That's what this book is for. To let you see what's possible.

The original book, preserved in Part Two, represents where I was in 2005. Some resources are dated. Some information has evolved. But the core truths—about the power of story, about fighting on three fronts of body, mind, and spirit—those haven't changed.

Read Part Two with compassion for who I was then, and with discernment about what still applies now. Part Three offers updated resources for today.

I cannot know how many people I have inspired to take hope. I don't live in the stories. They are just experiences I have had. They are here to be shared.

Leon told me to tell my story. I'm still telling it.

My work here on this planet is not yet done.

Neither is yours.

৶

# PART TWO

*The Original Edition*

*First published in 2006*

## Important Medical Disclaimer

The information contained in this book is based solely on the author's personal experience with cancer and her individual healing journey. It is provided for educational and informational purposes only.

The author is not a physician, and nothing in this book should be construed as medical advice, diagnosis, or treatment. The practices, protocols, and approaches described herein reflect one person's experience and may not be appropriate for anyone else.

Before making any changes to your diet, exercise routine, supplements, or medical treatment, you should consult with a qualified healthcare professional. Do not disregard professional medical advice or delay seeking treatment because of something you have read in this book.

Every person's situation is unique. What worked for the author may not work for you. Results vary, and no specific outcomes are guaranteed or implied.

The author and publisher disclaim any liability arising directly or indirectly from the use of this book.

# Battlefield Hope

*Lessons, Practices, and Resources to Help Fight Disease*

By Susan Brearley

## Dedication and Thanks

Thank you to everyone who read this material before release. I am so grateful for all your comments and assistance in helping with the birth. Thanks, too, for all those whom I have met on the journey. Without you, this work would not have been possible.

Dedicated to the great loves of my life today—the inspiration for my battle—my children, Sean and Russell, and my daughter-in-law, Terri, an amazing woman, who has also gifted us all with a granddaughter—Z.

With eternal gratefulness to my parents and grandparents, and Lucia, all of whom have gifted me with roots and wings.

❧

# Introduction

I recently passed through an airport lounge and wandered past a bookstore. I've had to stop buying books since it's become such a runaway habit that if I began reading now, non-stop to the end of my life, I don't know that I could finish all I've collected. But I digress. I scanned over the books, and seeing the dozens of self-help titles, each proclaiming to have the answer for how to have a perfect life, I pondered over the wonder that there doesn't exist even more confusion in the world than already does. And so, I could just as easily talk myself into abandoning all hope that anything might have to say in a book (about hope) would serve to stir the pot all the more. The world is already such a noisy place; perhaps, I speculated, I would serve it better in silence. But I recalled my encounter with Leon.

Leon was a very tall, very muscular, very dark-skinned man whom I met about ten years ago in Miami. I was speaking to a group of people there about my experience with cancer. I must have been somewhat tentative about what happened to me. I am convinced that there must have rung some truth of inspiration in the words I spoke that caused Leon, after dinner, in the restaurant parking lot, to confront me with the words "TELL YOUR STORY". I was so alarmed at being given this directive, especially since I'd already been thinking I WAS telling my story. I began to examine the message I carried, and what a gift it was for people to receive it. I also examined how I was delivering the message.

This book is the result of the encouragement of the many people I have come in contact with over the past ten years, who have traveled with me and who have told me that my story inspired them.

I have written each chapter with a specific theme, and the book has NO chronological organization per se, such that you can read any chapter based upon the title that attracts you to it. Each themed chapter consists of four parts. Part one, a story, which I hope will create a mind space for you that allows for personal contemplation and inspiration. Part two is a life lesson, but this will be the life lesson that I have gotten from the experience, and may not be so for you—you may receive a different inspiration than I have, or none at all. That is fine—there is no right or wrong in what you get. The third part is a practice. It is designed to be something simple that you can meditate on, contemplate in your daily life, and use as a help on your journey. Part four will give you additional resources you may find useful.

The ultimate purpose of this book is to help you heal, and healing happens on three fronts—body, mind, and spirit. A chair needs a minimum of three legs to stand. To win the battle against disease, you need all three strengthened and even, so you can be poised and ready on a field of hope.

My desire for all who read this book is that it serves to help transform your life such that you can realize the greatest possibilities you can imagine for yourself.

Good health to you!

*Susan B—January 22, 2005*

*Mohonk Mountain House*

*New Paltz, New York*

છ

# Practices

*Practice makes perfect.*

Having been raised with Pennsylvania Dutch parents in Berks County, PA, it was a phrase I heard frequently. And so I practiced. I practiced piano, trumpet, and guitar. I practiced dance—tap, ballet & jazz, though tap became my favorite. I practiced being a good Girl Scout. I practiced housekeeping. Later, I practiced having relationships—not very successfully, in my early estimations. Many serious relationships and three husbands later, I'd now say that all my relationships were successful, because each contributed to who I am today.

My third husband, Jeff, and I had an ongoing debate about practicing—although we did not call it such. We spoke about our fundamental natures—he as a 'be'-er and I as a 'do'-er. I am in action nearly constantly. He wanted to just 'be', no matter what that entails. He was always happier sitting and reflecting than being in action. It is an effort for me to have a sustained period of inactivity. I may be just as reflective as he is, but I have a need to be in action while doing the reflective work. It is easier for me to meditate while walking or dancing than while sitting.

When I was in IBM sales training, twenty years ago, my Dallas roommates called me the 'tornado'. They loved how I had so much energy the day after a late-night event. I'd zip around the condo, cleaning and tidying up.

I asked Jeff what he practices, and he said 'breathing'. And 'loving you'. For me, a practice exists very much in the physical; for him, it exists very much in the emotional and metaphysical.

My parents were familiar with farm life, but I didn't grow up on a farm. My mom had that experience, and so did my grandmother. They lived practical lives, their greatest concerns being simple ones—food, shelter, and clothing. They were much loved and taught to be reverent. Farm life was challenging, but rewarding. There was little time for play or frivolity. Life could be difficult if the weather was bad or problems occurred with food crops or animals, and relationships in a family group were focused on teamwork to produce the desired outcomes. In short, survival was the name of the game.

To have the luxury of time in which to read, keep a journal, sketch in a sketchbook, dance, sing, and play seemed to be a first gift in my family to my generation. Not having much of a guide in my natural family for these idle pastimes, I searched for guidance in books (they called me 'the bookworm' in my youth), with school friends, with neighbors. At 19, I sold all my belongings and drove my 1967 Volkswagen Beetle to New York to go to college.

I wanted to be a writer. A dear friend and neighbor in Pennsylvania, Lucia, read some of my early journaling—stream of consciousness meanderings mostly, with no particular point—and politely told me that if I wanted to be a writer, I should go out into the world and experience it. Go practice being human—I suppose that would be another way she could have phrased it. That was my intention when I set off for New York.

I thought I would go to school and study journalism. A reputable university offered me scholarship money, and that, along with a budding new relationship that began at the Philadelphia Folk Festival, lured me to New York.

Many folks have told me that I was so courageous to leave home at such a young age. Courage is when you know what it is that you are up against, and you proceed nonetheless. No, I operated out of pure naiveté in those days.

The cost of living in New York was exorbitant compared to simple Berks County life.

And I had another concern—a young son, whom I'd given birth to in 1975, when I was just 18. I attempted to piece together how I would pay for daily stipends for both of us and attend school full-time, but could not manage it. New York institutions were no help—after all—with only a few months in the state—I was still considered a Pennsylvania resident.

I applied to a large newspaper publishing conglomerate for a job, thinking that surely they would recognize the inherent talent that existed in my 'portfolio'—the year's worth of columns I had written and edited for the community college newspaper, which I had resurrected while studying there for an Associate Degree in Humanities. The Newspaper Group's bureaucratic processing must have interfered—they never called me for an interview. Desperate for work and money, I moved from reading their bylines to their classifieds.

Work in New York started for me on a jobber's assembly line. It was tedious in the routine, broken only by the rotation of what product we'd be packaging that day—toothpaste, moustache wax, or shampoo. Lunch time was the highlight. I worked beside a woman from India, who was so happy to have a job where, as she put it, she could 'pass time, make money'. In India, she shared with me that her prospects for employment were not nearly as good as working in her current job. She cooked her own lunches, and we would sit outside under a tree on the lawn, and she would share with me her fresh chapattis, dal, and savory specialties each day. It was my first introduction to Indian cuisine, and I loved it.

She invited me to her house for dinner one evening, where she showed me how to cook the chapattis. I was fascinated—no pans, just hand-rolled and placed directly on the open flame of her gas stove top. She had three sons, all studying to be doctors or lawyers, and I met them all as we shared a meal. I was intimidated by the power I felt in their presence of being. But I thought it odd that the whole male family ate their meal while transfixed to a TV set.

I resolved to always do my best, so that I could advance myself and be paid more than minimum wage. It was that sweet Indian woman who encouraged me that I could do so. I wondered out loud to her why she did not do the same. I felt a sense of loyalty to her and her kindness; a feeling that I wanted to take her hand and have her travel with me on my journey. She was happy in her place and station in life, and made it quite plain to me that she needed little else. When I told her that I had found a new position, she was happy for me. I was sad to say goodbye to her.

I worked for a family business next. They were abusive to their non-family employees, and according to employee rumors, were blacklisted by some employment temporary agencies. I stayed there one year, wanting to build a work profile and resume—I'd decided that would enhance my marketability.

It was a temporary agency that eventually placed me at IBM in 1981, as a receptionist and secretary. Hired in 1982, I self-trained to become a programmer; IBM invested in me to become a systems engineer and subsequently a sales rep. I've since held positions with them in marketing and communications.

Oddly enough, in the communications position—the one job function I performed nearly twenty years after applying to be a newspaper reporter, the one job that most closely resembled that job I aspired to at an early age—that job I wanted with the tight deadlines, constant hunts for exciting and relevant copy, and all the politics that anyone could ever hope for—I learned that I really didn't enjoy the job very much once I finally got it.

**Life Lesson:**

If you don't know where you are going, any road will take you there. Even if you think you know where you are going and believe you got off the path, you are on the path you need to be on anyway.

**Practice:**

Ask yourself some questions about what it is you practice in your life. It is in these repetitive practices that the essence of your life's work is revealed. Awareness of your own daily practices and knowing that you are at the source of choosing to keep those as your daily practices is foundational to what path you find yourself traveling.

**Resources:**

*For the mind:*

>Alice in Wonderland by Lewis Carroll

>The Narnia Series by CS Lewis

>What the Bleep do we Know? DVD

>Waking Life DVD

>The Biology Of Belief by Bruce Lipton

*For the emotions:*

>Emotional Release Therapy by Walter Weston

*For the spirit:*

>The religious text of your choice

>Prayer is Good Medicine by Larry Dossey

>Zen Keys by Thich Nhat Hanh

>Zen Philosophy, Zen Practice by Theich Thieen-Ean

*For the body:*

>Yoga: The Spirit and Practice of Moving into Stillness

# Telling Stories

The storytelling tradition—the oral tradition of sharing about ourselves and our cultures is as old as we are. It was our primary method of communicating, and as the language developed. Storytelling, in fact, since pictures predate language. Sharing a thought or idea with another person is an experience that binds us together in the common experience of being human.

When we are able to make a point to someone else about our experience, and when the other person is open to accepting that information, a great 'aha' moment can exist. It is the moment when two can become one and experience is shared. It is a moment that people search for in life and want to feel more of—we all want to be heard and to feel connected to others. That sense of 'belonging' drives much of the human experience.

But the sharing of an experience—the telling of our stories—does much more than just connect us.

I can remember times when my mother told stories—about her upbringing, her family, about when we were children growing up—about good times and bad times. Each time she told a story, I grew to memorize the exact words, and over time, I grew weary of hearing the same stories over and over. I wanted to leave and develop my own experiences so I could tell my own stories.

It took me many years to understand that my mother's telling stories was a way for her to share, an opportunity to connect with another—and the reason she told the same stories since I lived with her, and heard the same stories over and over—to others they were hearing those stories for the first time—and for her it was a way to sort through the many people she met in hopes of finding the one or ones that she could have that 'aha' moment with—the 'I GET IT—I GET YOU' of a shared moment and shared experience.

Self-help groups are wonderful for creating a safe environment where anyone can tell their story and connect with others who have had a similar experience. There are as many groups out there as there are human issues. I even found a 'Liars Anonymous' on the internet. You can Google anything, and chances are good you'll find a group that interests you.

There is more than just the creation of a shared experience in telling stories. There is also a personal freedom in telling, and 'releasing' a story. We are often 'trapped' within our story. We often believe that there is something in our life that repeats over and over again, and we also often believe that 'thing', and we get confused about why that should be. We live a life 'trapped' in this story that we tell others, as well as ourselves. When we can tell our story with an intention to 'release' it—such that it has no power over us anymore—then storytelling takes on a whole new dimension and purpose in our lives. This release can be achieved through other mediums as well and is the basis for all great artistic expression.

After my cancer diagnosis in 1995, my prognosis was not good. I was diagnosed with inflammatory breast cancer, and it was stage 3, borderline stage 4. Stage 4 is the final stage where the cancer has spread throughout the body. I had lymph involvement—I had a breast removed, and of the 32 lymph nodes taken from under my arm, 28 tested positive for cancer. Statistics said that for my rare type of cancer, for how fast it moved, and for the stage, I could have 6 months to a year to live. I had just given birth to my second son in March, and this was December. He was only 8 months old. I had much to live for, and resolved I would live to see my sons married. But that meant I had to get serious about focusing on my health, which had seriously run down after years of a hard-charging sales and marketing career.

I had an 'autologous bone marrow' procedure done. The stem cell was like a bone marrow transplant, but really a bone marrow 'rescue'.

First, I got hooked up to a machine that acts like dialysis, but for blood. Takes out blood in one tube and returns it in another. Harvest stem cells, then they clean them and freeze them.

Then, I went into the hospital for 30 days. Into a room on a totally sterile floor—HEPA filters everywhere. There I got bombarded with HIGH DOSES of chemo—so high that it destroyed my bone marrow.

When my blood counts were 0—and I basically had NO immune system left—they gave me back my stem cells. They are the 'grandmother' cells that evolve (in a short time) into red and white blood cells and platelets. I don't know how the cells know which are which, but they just know, and the stem cells take over while the bone marrow then reconstructs itself.

It was totally an experimental procedure. Very scary—during the time when there was no immune system in my body—basically, I had no blood defenses—I was at risk of overwhelming infection. I could easily have died. I knew that. But something inside me told me that whether I lived or died, everything would be OK.

And here I am, 10 years later. Thank God.

I was blessed to have a great support network. I was on prayer chains around the world. I did a lot of praying myself. I took a year off work so I could focus on staying alive. I luckily found a medical oncologist who was willing to work with me as a partner and not a dictator. She has since become a dear and trusted friend. I aggressively read and researched everything I could to develop a custom plan for my survival. I include that plan at the end of this book.

After a year had passed, I began to get stronger, and it became evident that I was NOT going to die; many people began to ask me what I had done. I began to share my story, my results, and give thanks to, above all, my maker. And I continued my education, further studying nutrition and iridology—the study of the iris of the eye as a tool to see the health of the body.

Iridology is a relatively new method—and similarly to how chiropractic was not well understood in its early days—it is still not widely known or respected. However, I have seen through many eyes the proof of advanced holistic iridology theory—that there is not just a physical component to illness but also an emotional component.

When we hold on to our stories, when we leave events incomplete with those we care about and love, when we choose not to say the words that we wish we would have said all along—that holding on selfishness can create its own emotional toxin that can have as

59

powerful an effect, or even more powerful than, the effect of the many toxins we ingest in the form of chemical additions in our food and drink.

**Life Lesson:**

Through the sharing of words and other media, it is possible to release a hold that the past may have over us, thereby contributing to new healing.

**Practice:**

Explore those stories that feel unresolved for you. Keep in mind that your view may not be exactly how an event occurred. Check in with others involved in your stories to get their view. RELEASE the story by sharing your view with others who can help you see how it actually happened, and allow that story to no longer have any power over you. Remember that in the release of any toxin, there is often a period where you feel worse rather than better. Keep your support group close to you, and if you don't have a group, find or build one for yourself.

**Resources:**

*For the mind:*

> The movie BIG FISH
>
> Healing and the Mind by Bill Moyers
>
> Self-Nurture by Domar and Dreher

*For the emotions:*

> Your Life as Story by Tristine Rainer

Writing the Sacred Journey by Elizabeth Andrew

Writing as a Way of Healing by Louise DeSalvo

*For the spirit:*

Stories of the Spirit, Stories of the Heart by Feldman and Kornfield

# The Power of Words

*"Give me a break."*

I had a habit of saying this expression from time to time. Being frustrated with people would urge it forth. Frustration with someone's choice to live unconsciously, or their choice to refuse to take responsibility for their actions, could summon up the phrase.

I began to notice I was using the phrase more often than usual. Then, I began to notice that I chipped three teeth (and a cap became dislodged) all over a 2-week period. I pointed out this observation to Jeff. We looked into each other's eyes, and I caught that elf-like glint which is so characteristic of when we shared an unspoken 'knowing' moment, and we burst out laughing. HA! I was asking for it!

Childlike, I immediately covered my tracks and loudly proclaimed, with his coaching, "Keep me WHOLE"!

Now, some might say this experience lives in the realm of superstition. I propose that we choose the path we walk, either consciously or unconsciously, and that our language shapes the environment we pass as we journey.

When I first moved to New York, in my early twenties, I met a woman whom I supposed, at the time, was in her late forties. Her name was Apple. She had beautiful, long, silver hair and fantastic, sparkling eyes. The energy in her body was effervescent, and there could be no doubt, in speaking with her, that she harbored a heart of gold. We did not share any business transactions, and we didn't spend much time together. But I was as sure as anyone could be of anyone else's, and we only shared a few brief conversations. I think she has come by her name because she really was the apple of the eye— beautiful, authentic, loving, resonating with the kind of energy you get when you hold or eat a perfect apple.

I recall beholding her, thinking, and declaring that I wanted to be as beautiful as I believed her to be when I became aged.

Now I am not an authority on most things, though I believe I know a little about many things. And I am not an authority on beauty, though I believe I feel it thoroughly when I am in its presence. When I look in the mirror today, I'm still pleased at what I see. Others kindly tell me that I am beautiful. And so, perhaps I am. I do know that the declaration I made in that small interaction I had with Apple continues to manifest itself, and I am ever so grateful I made it. I am sure others are the beneficiaries—I'm grateful to be able to give that kind of gift to others.

In my late teens, life seemed so difficult (as it does for many teens). I did not feel that I belonged to any peer group, and that is a precarious position to be in for any young adult. I seemed to get along well enough with everyone, but had no close friends—people whom I believed I could share absolutely anything with, and do so safely. I smoked cigarettes, experimented with drugs, played up against the societal boundaries by hitch-hiking, running away from home, learning about, and committing civil disobedience when a large concern (a nuclear power plant) threatened to come into our pristine environment and spoil it all. It seemed a glamorous and purposeful life. It made me feel alive—having a purpose. I wasn't sure exactly what my purpose was, but I did think that 'causes' contributed to my purpose somehow. So I drifted from cause to cause, meeting people and experiencing life.

I remember at one point making a declaration that wherever my life took me, I would look back at my life, from my deathbed, and have absolutely no regrets. I was, in those early years, as a piece of driftwood in an ocean current, rough edges being softened, beautiful grains being enhanced and pronounced, moving as the tides, predictable to watch for those accustomed to studying the tidal tables, but for one not familiar with the pattern, wondering why I kept passing some of the same familiar landmarks repeatedly.

On a trip to Mohonk Mountain House, I returned from a walk to Skytop, passing several couples making their pilgrimage to the pinnacle. One couple was friendly, and we briefly chatted—"it's worth the walk"—I encouraged them, and they lit up with anticipation of what was to come. I recognized a small piece of fulfillment in my early 'no regrets' declaration. Here I was, in this most beautiful, awe-inspiring result of our Creator's hand, and I was so appreciative of the wonder on the path.

I went to a Landmark Education seminar in New York City once. The weather was coming—a snowstorm. Instead of taking a train home, a friend and I drove home with two other participants. We all lived in the same general area. We anticipated the storm's approach. I confidently declared to the entire car—no, it will not snow. And it didn't. For a full 24 hours, we waited for the snow. It was everywhere—all around us, but it was not snowing in our county, and one that is known for getting heavy snows when others in our area often get little or none. I thought it so odd, and felt responsible for the clarity and stillness in the air. When the storm finally came, it enveloped us, dumping tremendous volumes of crystalline white powder. I felt relieved. I couldn't help wondering how I might have had on someone I had never met. In my responsibility, I decided not to make too many comments about the weather in the future.

I have come to feel reverence for that which must have embodied the ancient peoples who were called rainmakers.

**Life Lesson:**

When you are a person of your word, your words need not be numerous to positively affect your environment.

**Practice:**

Notice the words you speak, as you speak them. What might you be saying that you don't really intend? Some phrases we say because we learned them from others, but we don't really know why we say them. Practice trying on a new way of communicating your messages to others, without using the same phrases you always did. Start a journal. It's one of the best ways to visually examine how your words come out, before you say them.

**Resources:**

*For the mind:*

>Principles of Personal Integrity by Napoleon Hill

*For the emotions:*

>Emotional Intelligence by Daniel Goleman

>Energy Healing for Beginners by Ruth White

*For the spirit:*

>There's a Spiritual Solution to Every Problem by Dr. Wayne Dyer

*For the body:*

>Soothing music for meditation and healing

# The Truth

Who can say what the truth is? Many take the position that they know what it is, and can clearly state it.

Dear reader, I will only share with you my own experiences and observations. To me, what is true is something that resonates for me—like a sound wave inside a guitar that rings sweetly and perfectly—it is something that is not difficult to detect, on a large scale.

When we share experiences with each other, whatever we thought was holding us back in the story about that experience has no more power over us. And when others hear our experiences, they often discover that moment where we as humans all experience and witness the same observations.

We all have cancer cells, but our immune system is designed to handle anomalies in the body. But what happens when our system becomes weakened? Naturally, it works less well, less efficiently. How can it become weakened? Stress.

When the words we speak and the thoughts we think do not coincide, we are out of harmony. Our physical, emotional, and spiritual states are fractured. When in this place of disharmony, it is a likely time when the physical body, under stress from the disharmony, can be susceptible to illness.

This is an area of opportunity for us—a place where, once we can notice it, identify it, name it, we can work to heal to bring ourselves into alignment and restore our integrity. We'll explore that in the next few chapters. How does the healing happen?

My experience with cancer and degenerative disease began much earlier than I ever imagined. I'd been experiencing IBS and digestive disorders since I was very young. No one knew what they were, or acknowledged the possibility that there could be something that the physical was somehow more in control of the spiritual world. But to do so would be to admit that just because you can't see something (like the internal workings of a body, or magnetic forces, or gravity, or the hand of the Creator) doesn't mean that any of them don't exist.

# Giving and Receiving

I recently shared a moment with one of the culinary students renting a room in my home. We were talking about our 9/11 experiences. Both of us agreed that it was one of the most emotional experiences of our lives.

I told him that I was so overwhelmed with emotion when I saw the first tower toppling down, live, on network TV, that I ran to my bedroom, fell to my knees, and began to pray to God to make it stop! Similarly, he cried over the travesty of so much senseless death. How could humanity treat itself in this way?

I read to him a portion of the introduction to Thich Nhat Hanh's book 'Zen Keys'. In it, Philip Kapleau speaks of how the ego gets in the way of our shared experience, and how our view of a dualistic world—an us-versus-them perspective—in which we believe that we are actually separate from the world, is the largest cause of our suffering. And I would add, our misunderstandings of each other.

When we give of ourselves, even when, and especially when, supremely challenged to do so, we receive gifts tenfold. They aren't always the gifts we ask for, and they come in unexpected ways. But there are some laws of the universe that remain unaltered.

I loved an expression I heard in a Landmark education session—'we aren't human beings having a spiritual experience, we are spiritual beings having a human experience'.

He and I live on the top of a small mountain. We are surrounded by nature. It is peaceful and beautiful, and the rhythms of nature are all around us. If we were able to leave our bodies and observe what happened here, very little would change. The sun would still rise and set, the rabbits would still munch the clover, the turkeys and deer would still convene and browse. Why do we insist that our very presence makes ALL the difference in what happens? It is for us to enjoy, appreciate, love, and experience.

**Life Lesson:**

Prayer is good medicine, and it is one of the rare things in the human experience that is free! When we give of ourselves to others, our thoughts and words, whether those thoughts and words are in the spirit world or the flesh, we release a gift to them.

**Practice:**

Pray. Talk to your makers, to nature, to the wonders and mysteries of the universe. Talk to your ancestors. It is known that prayer affects the brain and the body in ways that are yet not fully understood by science. Miracles can and do happen every day. The first step in experiencing them is to be open to the idea that they surround us.

**Resources:**

*For the mind:*

> Miracles by Stuart Wilde

> Miracles by C. S. Lewis

> Miracles Can Be Yours Today by Pat
Robertson

*For the spirit:*

> Tibetan Meditation by Tarthang Tulku

*For the body:*

> The pH Miracle by Robert and Shelly Young

# Image

When people see me on the street, if I can catch their eye, I smile at them. It's the rare person who won't smile back. I wonder about what they think I'm up to. Without a conversation, I'll never know.

Before my cancer experience, I had long, beautiful hair. I was asked to be a hair model for some occasions by my hairdresser, so full and handsome were my locks.

The receptionist who staffed the front desk at the salon where I had my hair styled was absolutely gorgeous. When I would appear for my appointments, I would imagine what kind of glamorous life she must certainly be living. Great joy and fortune must surely go hand in hand with great beauty.

After my cancer diagnosis, there was barely any time to think. So aggressive was this inflammatory breast cancer, within one week, I was in surgery. The doctors insisted that an immediate mastectomy was a certain requirement to save my life. With no time to research the alternatives, and definitely no time to ponder or argue, I took their advice.

I had a doctor who I firmly believe is the world's best. She did research on my behalf, did battle with insurance companies on my behalf, and sent tissue samples to labs for testing outside the boundaries of what traditional therapies demanded. She was like a Gil Grissom of the oncological lab—dedicated, determined, relentless, and professional. In her great wisdom, she did not utter a prognosis—or any proclamations about where I was headed. What doctor has the right to play God in that way? With what certainty can they decide on a patient's behalf?

Years after my cancer recovery, considered by all a remarkable event, I contemplated the many ways in which I could return my appreciation for the miracle of my life each new day. I had a vision of myself, lying down, with hundreds of arms below me (like a strange scene from a techno modern dance club), lifting me up. I saw a hand reach out of the sky and touch me. And in that touch, somehow, I knew that no matter what happened, whether I lived or died, everything would be alright and was as it was meant to be.

And then a miracle happened. I recovered. Slowly and painfully. My husband told me my eyes were yellow. I vomited blue stuff. It was incredible.

At one point, when I began to eat solid food again (I hadn't eaten for a month), I realized that I couldn't taste my food. OH, the agony of that. I thought, 'I cannot live without taste buds!' What a cruel thing—to have everything taste like cardboard the rest of my life. I asked the doctor about that. She admitted that, yes, it was a side effect of the chemo, and my taste buds might come back.

I had to come to terms with that. So, I prayed some more. And I said, 'ok, fine, if that's the way it is, then so be it. I am happy to have my life, no matter what.' And the NEXT DAY, a miracle happened. I could taste my food again.

**Life Lesson:**

Sometimes we want something so badly that it is impossible to possess it. The universe just won't allow it. But when we can relax and release our ego-inspired desires and wants, miracles can occur, and gifts appear.

**Practice:**

What is it that you hold onto and refuse to let go of? What do you think you cannot live with or do without?

**Resources:**

*For the mind:*

Love, Medicine and Miracles by Bernie Siegel

Anatomy of Hope by Jerome Groopman

*For the emotions:*

Healing Through the Dark Emotions by Miriam Greenspan

Healing for Damaged Emotions by David Seamands

*For the body:*

The Miracle of the Breath by Andy Caponigro

101 Miracles of Natural Healing by Luke Chan

Breast Cancer Options website: breastcanceroptions.org

# Healing
You have made the decision to heal. Now what?

Is there time? Is it too late? Can anything happen? Can miracles happen? I worked with an herbologist—a man whose family lineage in herbology pre-dates the Christian Bible—who said that healing for serious disease is like sitting on a fence. It is easy to fall off the fence on either side.

I cannot say what is, or will be true for you. I can tell you what worked for me. I am 10 years past a diagnosis and prognosis that, had I paid too much attention to the associated science and numbers, I might not be here today.

I will not disagree that the medical care I received was of tremendous value. But I believe that the whole package—everything I did—contributed to my being here today. I changed my diet. I alkalized my body chemistry through a combination of foods and herbs. I was accepted into the hospital, and I was given ultra-high doses of chemo and no radiation. I underwent an autologous stem cell procedure. I had a mastectomy. I eliminated spurious chemicals in my surroundings. I eliminated toxic agents to my emotions and spirit. I prayed and was on many prayer chains. I thank God today that I availed myself of everything available to me to fight the disease. I am ever vigilant.

At one point early on in the process, I realized that I might not live. I went into the hospital for 30 days for the stem cell procedure. This procedure is tough stuff. Sometime before it began, or so in advance, I was hooked up to a machine—dialysis of sorts—that removes blood and separates cells; they collect stem cells, clean and freeze them.

During that time, I recognized that I might not make it. I understood that I could die there in the hospital. I made peace with that. I had a vision of myself, lying down, with hundreds of arms below me (like a strange scene from a techno modern dance club), lifting me up.

Herring's Law of Healing states that the body heals 1) from the top down, 2) from the inside out, and 3) in the reverse order in which it became ill.

To me, this means that 1) Your brain and its thoughts will be the ultimate control point for how you heal and how fast you heal. Your motivation to be well—your desire to live or die—your reasons for living—all affect your healing, at a cellular level. It is well known that laughter has a powerful healing effect on the body. Why? It puts the brain and its thoughts in a positive place.

2) As a zygote in the womb, those tiny cells begin to differentiate. The very first identifiable structure in a human embryo is called the gut tube. It becomes the intestinal tract. From that tube emerge major organs and eyes. Everything is covered with a membrane, which is the same as what covers the gut tube. From inside the womb, everything in the body is connected via the intestinal tract and the eyes.

3) Just as Hansel and Gretel had to come out of the woods to come back to their pristine original home, we have a walk to come back from serious illness. And along the way, when we begin to heal, we pass the same breadcrumbs—the same landmarks—the same

symptoms—which we experienced on the way into that house of illness.

Expecting to start a regimen of healing means buckling up your seatbelt. Often, people I work with when I do 'cleansing coach' work, share with me the symptoms of something they had forgotten all about, because it was a symptom they passed many years earlier, and had disappeared when a new, more severe symptom appeared. I am happy to report that I no longer experience IBS symptoms—but it took many years for them to completely disappear. The rule of thumb in healing is that it takes 1 month of cleansing for every 6 months that the problems have existed. Imagine if you have experienced symptoms of degeneration of one form or another for 50 years—it would take 100 months of cleansing to get the body into a pristine condition again! And sometimes the body is SO stressed and SO toxic that the cleansing process is painful, challenging, and difficult. Who wants to reexperience symptoms that they thought were long gone? The major question in healing is—do you want to live? Or are you ready to die? I believe, as did many indigenous peoples, that this is a choice YOU make, and not the doctors.

**Life Lesson:**

Healing happens. It's a miracle we were all born with. We see it every day when we cut ourselves, and the cut heals. It isn't something that is dictated.

**Practice:**

Think of the body as the house—the temple of your spirit. In what condition have you kept your home? How much time do you spend in reverence and care of your brick-and-mortar house? How much time do you spend on the care of your physical body?

Examine the products you eat—read the labels. If it's got chemical additives and you don't know what they are, don't eat them. Consumer Reports, in two separate issues, verified that non-organic fruits and veggies have pesticides all over them. Choose and eat organics. Find a local CSA (community supported agriculture projects) for clean sources of food. Filter your drinking water with a Multipure filter. Our ancestors didn't use all the chemical cleaners we allow into our houses today. Switch to non-toxics. Use vinegar, baking soda, and lemon juice. Eliminate the emotional toxins. Find a coach who can help you identify those toxins in your life if you are overwhelmed with the project. Use Herring's Law of Healing as a guide.

**Resources:**

*For the mind:*

> Custom Medical Research
> http://www.thehealthresource.com/

*For the emotions:*

> Byron Katie's work
> http://www.thework.com/

*For the body:*

> CSA references www.nal.usda.gov/afsic/csa/

> Bernard Jensen Foundation resource:
> www.bernardjensen.org/

# Science

I feed the birds. I love to watch them and their high-spirited antics. And gradually, humans have encroached on the birds' natural habitat, which makes their ability to forage more and more difficult each year. So I give back to them by feeding them, and they give me great joy.

We have many squirrels. Frankly, we are overrun. They can empty my feeders in a single day. And they are very destructive.

I put out a have-a-heart trap, and there are so many, I can trap 3-4 squirrels a day. That's a LOT of squirrels. I drive them across the river. It's my own relocation program. I know they won't swim back.

Over the course of several days, I watched this one very clever squirrel. I got to know them by their size and shape, and the way their fur appeared, or the thickness or thinness of their tails. I could easily see which ones were male or female. This one was a male, older, wiser. I had just installed the ultimate in squirrel-proof feeders. It worked wonderfully—for 99% of the squirrels. But this clever one—he was not giving up. I watched him contort his body over and over, persistently trying every configuration of legs and feet and mouth and tail he could. Days went by. And then, a miracle happened. He figured out how to get in there.

The feeder operated on a pressure switch. It was also positioned in a way that if a squirrel were to hang on it in any manner, it shut automatically. This squirrel figured out, through trial and error, that if he adjusted the amount of pressure he placed on this bar, the opening would not close all the way, and he could reach inside and get out the nuts he coveted. That's the day I became a squirrel trapper.

It's also the day I thought to myself—' how different is our modern science from the brain of a squirrel?' Everything that happens in science and medicine is a 'trial'—the doctors 'practice'—the drug companies run 'trials'—and hopefully, we have no errors, at least not in the human population. But science is about hypothesis and trial and error, and in that regard, our modern methods of dealing with illness are primitive compared to our methods of assisting the body in its own inherent process of healing.

**Life Lesson:**

The time we live in affects our perspective of what could or should happen next. Your body heals no matter what era you are born into. We are lucky to be living in an age of advanced sanitation and medical science, yet there are those on the planet who have yet to experience those luxuries. Much of our increased lifespan has to do with improvements in sanitation. Whom do we thank for the miracles that occur in the world?

**Practice:**

Examine your view of how science affects your belief in what natural abilities your body already possesses. If you have a medical doctor, ask yourself what role they presently play in helping you heal. Are they partners, or are they dictators? What roles are you most comfortable with in that relationship? Do you believe in what you cannot see? Viruses and bacteria were impossible to see before the invention of the microscope. When science proves something to be true, does that make it untrue until the proof exists? Always thank the source of your blessings and gifts.

**Resources:**

*For the mind:*

First Pulse: A Personal Journey in Cancer Research by Dr. Merrill Garnett

The Healing Mind: The Vital Links between Brain and Behavior, Immunity and Disease by Paul Martin

*For the emotions:*

Molecules of Emotion: The Science Behind Mind Body Medicine by Candace Pert

*For the spirit:*

Being And Becoming: A Book Of Lessons In The Science Of Mind by Fenwick Holmes

*For the body:*

Evaluating Alternative Cancer Therapies by David J. Hess

High Level Wellness by Donald B Ardell

# Possibilities

The week I was diagnosed as having breast cancer, a letter was sent to my general practitioner. That week, he called me at home. He told me that he had cancer—childhood leukemia—and that he was very sick. They didn't think he would make it. But he did, and he has a wife and children, and an active medical practice.

That phone call gave me inspiration and the possibility of having hope. So did many other gifts of sharing from people along the way—the old woman in the church who took me aside and discreetly told me she was a breast cancer survivor, all the other women who came forward when I made it public about what I had, who shared their stories of triumph over illness.

My GP is a Doctor of Osteopathy—a D.O.—which is a nice cross between traditional medicine and a holistic naturopathic. Allopathic medicine is trained to 'isolate and treat'—hence, they treat symptoms, and not always whole body systems.

That takes constant vigilance and attention.

Anything is possible. I am living, breathing, and walking proof of that. I believe that miracles can and do happen all around us.

Hope is something we can choose to keep close to us. It is not anything that anyone has the right to take away from us. No one has the power to take it from us, unless we ALLOW them to do so. Even at the end of my life, I choose to keep hope as a treasure—one of many gifts that being alive and human give us.

**Life Lesson:**

The universe really does help those who help themselves. Too much activity can cause us to lose sight of what to give, and where to give, thanks for, and to. Too little activity and inertia can prevent us from helping ourselves. It's all about balance. Children are born with an inherent understanding of balance.

**Practice:**

Create a new habit. Take some moments for yourself every day. Say a prayer. Sit and listen to nature. Add some moments of silence to your day. Gather your thoughts— where you've been today, where you are now. Give thanks to the source of it all.

**Resources:**

*For the mind:*

> Stealth Health by Reader's Digest editors

> Motivational Practice by Rick Botelho

*For the emotions:*

> Why people get sick and why people get well by Joseph B Mitchell

## *For the spirit:*

Visit your favorite spa. Sit on your porch deck, or in your yard.

## *For the body:*

The Right Dose: How To Take Vitamins And Minerals Safely by Patricia Hausman MS

Your Body's Many Cries for Water by Dr. Batmanghelidj

# Moments of Silence

I was taking my son to school one day, and the topic of money arose. "Everything costs money," I told him, "nothing is free". He quickly responded. "Air is free". I said, "So far". He replied, "Life is free". I had no retort. I became silent and contemplative.

Even now, 10 years past my cancer diagnosis and treatment, I still get caught up in the hubbub of life, and with a single, simple statement, my 11-year-old son has the ability to stop me in my tracks and cause me to be thankful for life again.

After the first year had passed post-chemo, and it became apparent that the statistics were not applying to me, I started the habit of saying a prayer each day. It was very simple. I said, "Thank you for this day, and for every day you choose to gift me".

It is easy to get busy with the business of life, and forget to give thanks.

Yesterday, I got a notice of the death of a young woman whom I considered young and healthy. Complications from surgery. I only saw her 6 months ago. How fragile life is. We all leave sometime, and no one here on earth knows exactly when that will be.

**Life Lesson:**

Less is more. The universe really does help those who help themselves. Too much activity can cause us to lose sight of what to give, and where to give, thanks for, and to. Too little activity and inertia can prevent us from helping ourselves. It's all about balance. Children are born with an inherent understanding of balance.

**Practice:**

Create a new habit. Take some moments for yourself every day. Say a prayer. Sit and listen to nature. Add some moments of silence to your day. Gather your thoughts—where you've been today, where you are now. Give thanks to the source of it all.

**Resources:**

*For the mind:*

> www.landmarkeducation.com classes for safe sharing

*For the emotions:*

> www.oncochat.org - a website for all family members to share and be supported

*For the spirit:*

> spiritualresource.com

*For the body:*

> www.aforapple.com - a launching pad for healing the physical body

# Practices To Fight Disease

There are some basic premises that guided me in my battle against cancer.

1. The body knows how to heal itself.

2. Degenerative diseases like cancer live in acidic, low-oxygen environments and cannot thrive in highly oxygenated alkaline environments. Alkaline environments are the opposite of acidic environments.

3. Enzymes are sparks of life.

4. Water is fundamental to life. Water is fundamental to cleansing, second only to air.

5. Toxins interfere with the body's natural ability to heal quickly.

I very simply and only ate those foods that I knew would contribute to creating an alkaline condition. I avoided most meats. Studies in Scandinavia showed CoEnzyme Q10 helped women with breast cancer—I took the maximum safe dose. I took cleansing herbs to clean the GI tract, a major source of autointoxication. I washed all fruits and veggies with a wash, but mostly I bought all ORGANIC produce. Enzymes are destroyed by cooking foods—vitamins and minerals cannot work without enzymes—so I ate as much uncooked food as possible.

My doctor didn't like that I was using herbs and cleansing at the same time I was undergoing chemo. But I told her it was what I intended to continue to do. I cannot say if the chemo or my diet was the cause of my remarkable recovery—I'd be inclined to say both made contributions.

Should you choose to adopt a plan such as the one I used, do not do it without consulting with your medical doctor.

**What I did each day:**

Upon waking: A glass of water, preferably alkalized or distilled. Dry skin brush, then shower. 2-3 capsules of Experience cleanse from Awareness.

At breakfast: Any supplements - multivitamin, CoEnzyme Q10, etc. Fresh-squeezed citrus juice. Oatmeal or muesli (no boxed cereals). Carrot cocktail with parsley, apple, and cantaloupe. Any starches are WHOLE GRAINS only.

In the evening: Protein of choice - no red meat - fish, chicken, eggs. Fresh almonds & brazil nuts, a handful. Fresh water.

Before bedtime: 2-3 ounce cup of Floressence tea. 1-2 capsules of Experience digestive cleanse.

I drank plenty of water (from an alkaline source) to help the body eliminate toxins. I juiced at least 1 pound of carrots daily (my palms turned orange and my doctor was not happy with me, but I had read early published reports about live source vitamin A eliminating cancer in mice).

# PART THREE

*Resources for Today*

# A Note About Resources

Resources change. In the thirty years since my diagnosis, websites have come and gone, organizations have merged or dissolved, and entirely new categories of support have emerged. The alkaline water machine I imported from Japan in 1995 is now obsolete—you can buy alkaline water at any grocery store.

The resources listed in Part Two reflect what was available in 2005. Some of those websites no longer exist. Some of those phone numbers have changed. That's the nature of resources—they evolve as the world evolves.

What follows is a current snapshot of support available today. By the time you read this, some of these may have changed, too. Use this as a starting point, not an endpoint. The most important resource is your willingness to seek help and your determination to advocate for yourself.

I have not personally used all of these resources, but they come from reputable organizations with established track records. Always verify current information directly with the organization before relying on it.

## Cancer Organizations and Hotlines

These organizations provide information, emotional support, and connections to local resources. Most services are free.

### American Cancer Society

Comprehensive cancer information, support programs, and services, including lodging assistance (Hope Lodge) and transportation help. 1-800-227-2345, available 24/7. cancer.org

### Cancer Support Community

Free counseling, support groups, and education programs for anyone affected by cancer. Their Cancer Support Helpline offers emotional support and resource referrals. 1-888-793-9355, Monday–Friday 9 am–9pm ET. cancersupportcommunity.org

### CancerCare

Free professional counseling, support groups, educational workshops, and financial assistance for cancer-related costs. 1-800-813-4673. cancercare.org

### National Cancer Institute Cancer Information Service

Accurate, up-to-date information about cancer types, treatments, clinical trials, and coping. 1-800-422-6237 (1-800-4-CANCER). cancer.gov

## SHARE Cancer Support

Survivor-led support specifically for women with breast or ovarian cancer, available in English, Spanish, and twelve other languages. 1-844-275-7427. sharecancersupport.org

## Imerman Angels

Free one-on-one cancer support matches patients, survivors, and caregivers with someone who has faced the same type of cancer. imermanangels.org

## Gilda's Club / Cancer Support Community

Free support groups, workshops, and community programs are named for comedian Gilda Radner. Now part of Cancer Support Community with locations nationwide. cancersupportcommunity.org/find-location

## Online Communities

Connection with others who understand what you're going through can be invaluable. These communities let you connect on your own schedule, from anywhere.

### Cancer Survivors Network (American Cancer Society)

An online community where cancer survivors, families, and friends can share experiences, ask questions, and find support. csn.cancer.org

### MyLifeLine (Cancer Support Community)

Create a personal page to share updates with family and friends, reducing the exhaustion of repeating news. Also connects you with others facing similar diagnoses. mylifeline.org

### Inspire Cancer Communities

Disease-specific online support communities where patients and caregivers share experiences and information. inspire.com

### Stupid Cancer

Community specifically for young adults (ages 15-39) affected by cancer—a population with unique challenges. stupidcancer.org

## Meditation and Mindfulness Apps

Meditation helped me survive. These apps bring practices that once required in-person classes to your phone, available whenever you need them.

### CancerCare Meditation App

Free app created specifically for people affected by cancer, featuring guided meditation sessions, inspirational talks, and soothing music. Partnership between CancerCare and BodyMind Sessions. Available on iPhone; search CancerCare Meditation

### Calm

General meditation app with some cancer-specific content. Research shows it can reduce symptom burden in cancer patients. Features sleep stories, breathing exercises, and guided meditations. calm.com

### Insight Timer

Free meditation app with thousands of guided meditations, including many focused on healing, pain management, and coping with illness. insighttimer.com

### Headspace

Guided meditation app with programs for stress, sleep, and managing difficult emotions. Some hospitals offer free subscriptions to patients. headspace.com

### UCLA Mindful

Free app from UCLA's Mindful Awareness Research Center offering guided meditations, mindfulness exercises, and wellness tools developed by researchers. uclahealth.org/programs/marc

## Loving Meditations

Created by a caregiver and cancer survivor couple, featuring daily inspirations, guided meditations, breath work, and mindfulness-based stress reduction. lovingmeditations.com

## Books for Healing and Hope

These books have helped others facing serious illness find meaning, hope, and practical guidance.

### *Man's Search for Meaning by Viktor Frankl*

The Holocaust survivor and psychiatrist's exploration of finding purpose in suffering. Essential reading for anyone facing the impossible.

### *The Gift by Edith Eger*

Dr. Eger, a Holocaust survivor and student of Frankl, offers twelve transformative lessons about choosing freedom over victimhood.

### *When Breath Becomes Air by Paul Kalanithi*

A neurosurgeon's memoir about confronting his own mortality after a lung cancer diagnosis. Profound and beautifully written.

### *The Bright Hour by Nina Riggs*

A poet's luminous memoir about living with metastatic breast cancer, finding joy and meaning in ordinary moments.

### *Anticancer: A New Way of Life by David Servan-Schreiber*

A physician-researcher who survived brain cancer shares evidence-based approaches to nutrition, exercise, and emotional health.

## Wherever You Go, There You Are by Jon Kabat-Zinn

The classic introduction to mindfulness meditation, written by the founder of Mindfulness-Based Stress Reduction (MBSR).

## Being Mortal by Atul Gawande

A surgeon's thoughtful exploration of aging, dying, and how medicine can do better. Important for understanding end-of-life options.

*A note about books and healing – there are thousands of books I could personally recommend. A few years ago, I set a goal to read 200 books a year. Each time we read a book, we change inside. Our synapses rewire a bit. We get a new lens with which to see the world. Keep reading. The books you personally need are out there, and if you seek them, you will find them.*

# Financial Navigation and Assistance

Cancer can be expensive. These resources can help with treatment costs, living expenses, and navigating insurance.

## Cancer Financial Assistance Coalition (CFAC)

Coalition of organizations providing financial help to cancer patients. Their website links to multiple assistance programs. cancerfac.org

## Patient Advocate Foundation

Case managers help with insurance appeals, debt crisis, and job retention issues related to illness. 1-800-532-5274. patientadvocate.org

## HealthWell Foundation

Financial assistance for underinsured patients to cover copays, premiums, and other out-of-pocket costs. 1-800-675-8416. healthwellfoundation.org

## NeedyMeds

Database of patient assistance programs, free and low-cost clinics, and drug discount programs. needymeds.org

## PAN Foundation (Patient Access Network)

Helps underinsured patients with out-of-pocket costs for specific diseases. 1-866-316-7263. panfoundation.org

## Cancer Care Co-Payment Assistance Foundation

Helps with insurance co-payments for cancer treatment. cancercare.org

**Joe's House**

Helps cancer patients and families find affordable lodging near treatment centers. joeshouse.org

**Ronald McDonald House Charities**

Low-cost or free housing for families of children receiving cancer treatment. rmhc.org

# For Family Members and Caregivers

Cancer affects the whole family. Caregivers need support too.

## Caregiver Action Network

Education, peer support, and resources specifically for family caregivers. 1-855-227-3640. caregiveraction.org

## Family Caregiver Alliance

Support services, education, and advocacy for family caregivers. 1-800-445-8106. caregiver.org

## Well Spouse Association

Peer support for spouses and partners of chronically ill or disabled individuals. 1-732-577-8899. wellspouse.org

## Lotsa Helping Hands

Free online tool to coordinate meals, rides, and other help from your community. lotsahelpinghands.com

## CaringBridge

Free personal websites where families can post updates and receive support during a health journey. caringbridge.org

# Understanding Palliative Care and Hospice

These terms are often confusing. Understanding the difference matters.

Palliative care focuses on alleviating symptoms and enhancing the quality of life for individuals with serious illnesses. It can begin at diagnosis and continue alongside curative treatment. You do not have to be dying to receive palliative care. Research shows that patients who receive early palliative care often live longer and with a better quality of life.

Hospice care is for people whose illness is no longer responding to curative treatment and who are expected to live six months or less. Hospice focuses on comfort, dignity, and quality of life rather than curing the disease. It provides comprehensive support—medical, emotional, and spiritual—for both the patient and family. Most hospice care is provided at home.

All hospice care includes palliative care, but not all palliative care is hospice. Ask your doctor about palliative care early—don't wait until the end. It's an extra layer of support, not giving up.

## National Hospice and Palliative Care Organization

Information about hospice and palliative care, including a provider locator. 1-800-658-8898. nhpco.org

## GetPalliativeCare.org

Information and provider directory from the Center to Advance Palliative Care. getpalliativecare.org

## Practical Help

Sometimes you need help with the basics—transportation, food, and medication costs.

### Mercy Medical Angels

Help with transportation to medical appointments, including gas cards, bus fare, and airline tickets. mercymedical.org

### Road to Recovery (American Cancer Society)

Volunteer drivers provide free rides to cancer treatment. 1-800-227-2345

### Meals on Wheels

Delivers meals to homebound individuals. 1-888-998-6325. mealsonwheelsamerica.org

### RxAssist

Database of pharmaceutical assistance programs offering free or low-cost medications. rxassist.org

### 211

Dial 211 from any phone to connect with local resources for food, housing, utilities, and other basic needs. 211.org

# A Final Word

When I was diagnosed in 1995, I had to import an alkaline water machine from Japan. I had to track down obscure research papers. I had to find practitioners who would take me seriously.

You now have significantly more options available to you.

Use these resources. Ask for help. Build your team. You don't have to do this alone.

And remember—resources are just tools. The real resource is inside you—the will to fight, the capacity for hope, the ability to envision a future self and then reach for it.

That is what got me through. That is what will get you through too.

— *Susan Brearley*

# ABOUT THE AUTHOR

Susan Brearley is a two-time cancer survivor, writer, and practicing Buddhist who has been defying medical predictions since 1995.

Born in Reading, Pennsylvania, Susan began her career at IBM, where she spent 27 years in various roles, including programmer, systems engineer, and sales representative. A terminal cancer diagnosis at age 37 launched her on an unexpected journey of self-directed healing that combined Western medicine with nutrition, meditation, and an unwavering refusal to accept someone else's timeline for her life.

She first shared her story in the original Battlefield Hope, which was self-published in 2006. In the decades since, she has spoken to groups across the country, trained in iridology and natural health, and continued to write, publishing over 1,200 pieces on Medium.com across various topics, including food, wellness, Buddhism, and the writing life.

Susan holds a CNHP certification in natural health and studied advanced iridology with Dr. David Pesek. She also earned a bachelor's degree in psychology and Global Indigenous Knowledge Systems, a master's in organizational management and leadership, as well as certificates in Human System Dynamics and ICF coaching. Along with being a graduate of Scott Dikker's Comedy Business School, she also loves improv classes. She is Editor-in-Chief of multiple Medium.com publications and leads Wordsmiths' Weekly, a free Saturday writing workshop.

She currently lives in the Hudson Valley of New York, where she writes, teaches, operates an Airbnb, works at a local hospital, and continues to prove that life after a death sentence can be very long indeed.

Susan can be reached at Susan.Brearley@gardenofneuro.org.

She is available for speaking engagements.

෨

# OTHER WORKS BY THE AUTHOR

## Anthologies

A Safe and Brave Space

Emergent

Fine Linea

I Am From

The Talk

Wouldn't You Rather Be Laughing?

## By the author

Wordsmiths' Weekly: 500 Writers Prompts

## Edited by

The Lunchbox: A Collection of Short Stories

by A.L. Fredine

## COLOPHON

This book was set in Garamond,

a typeface originally designed by Claude Garamond

in sixteenth-century France.

The text was composed and designed by the author.

First published December 2025

by Garden of Neuro Institute Publishing

Printed in the United States of America

www.ingramcontent.com/pod-product-compliance
Lightning Source LLC
Chambersburg PA
CBHW031437270326
41930CB00007B/754